Hey, welcome to London, capital of the United Kingdom. It's a city packed with history, culture, and fun!

Take a tour on a bus that turns into a boat, whirl high in the sky on the London Eye, or explore the city on foot. Done that? Then experience a lesson in a Victorian school, watch a puppet show on a barge, get lost in a maze in Hampton Court, plunge into the rainforest at London Zoo, and much more. No wonder London is the second-most visited city in the world!

Well, what are you waiting for? Follow your guide dog, Go!

kidsGo! Travel Guides
Written by Mio Debnam
Illustrated by Tania Willis

HAVEN
BOOKS

Design Director: Timothy Jones / Designer: Katie Kwan
Published by Haven Books Limited, Hong Kong
ISBN 978-988-18967-4-2
Copyright © 2011 by Haven Books Limited
www.havenbooksonline.com

NOTE TO OUR READERS: We try to recommend the best
attractions, restaurants, and tour providers, using trusted
word-of-mouth recommendations; however, we cannot be held
responsible for the safety, scope and quality of their service.
We also strive to provide the most accurate information
possible, but of course, some things may have changed by
the time you visit. If you do notice anything inaccurate in our
guide, or think we've missed out on listing something really
good, please help us to make it better by letting us know about
it. We'd also love to hear from you about all the things you
liked or disliked during your trip, so we can continue to keep
our guides as up-to-date and reliable as possible.

How to tell us? Simply log on to the Family Feedback page at:
www.kidsgotravelguides.com

CONTENTS

BUCKINGHAM PALACE ✓

Buckingham Gate, Westminster SW1A

'Buck House' as the palace is sometimes called, is the home of the Queen. If you visit, take a look at the flagpole on top of the palace. If the Queen's flag – known as 'The Royal Standard' – is flying there rather than the more familiar Union Jack, it means the Queen is in town, although not necessarily at home that minute! During August and September, while she's away, you can take a tour of the staterooms, which are huge and full of ornate golden decorations, massive oil paintings and glittering chandeliers … or, if you don't have time to visit, you can go on a virtual tour on *www.royal.gov.uk* instead.

Remember to go to see the **Royal Guards**, before you leave. You'll find them standing in the sentry boxes by the main gate, or marching to and fro nearby. They're not allowed to talk, or even look at visitors. But they don't mind if you get up close to admire their red-jacketed uniforms and tall furry bearskin hats, or slip next to them for a quick photo! The **Changing of the Guard** ceremony, which takes place every day in the palace courtyard, is worth watching too (see pg 22).

MUST-DOS

HYDE PARK ✓

W2 🚇 Knightsbridge/S. Kensington/Lancaster Gate

If you're all shopped out in Knightsbridge, or you want a break from museum hopping in South Kensington (pg 33/34), head over to nearby Hyde Park. It has something for everyone: lots of paths to play squirrel-spotting on; two playgrounds for kids under 12 (one at Edinburgh Gate, near the **Mandarin Oriental Hotel**, Knightsbridge; and the other next to Westbourne Gate on the northwest corner of the park); miles of bridle-paths for horse riding (pg 19); and grassy areas where you can play Frisbee. There's even a sports center with tennis courts, a golf putting range and exercise equipment for people over 60!

And don't forget the **Serpentine**, the lake in the middle of the park. Between Easter and end of October, you can rent a rowing boat or pedal-boat to explore the lake. If you're feeling brave enough to swim in the cold and rather murky water, pull on your swimsuit and go to the Lido swimming area on the southern bank, where there is also a paddling pool for the little kids. When you get

> **Did you know?**
> Buckingham Palace has 775 rooms, including 78 bathrooms!

TOP SIGHTS &

tired and thirsty from all that activity, head over to one of the five refreshment points scattered around the park for an ice-cream or a drink. If you'd rather sit down and have something more filling, go to the **Serpentine Bar and Kitchen** (on the northeastern corner of the lake) or the café at the Lido swimming area.

THE LONDON EYE ✓

Riverside Building, County Hall, Westminster Bridge Road SE1 🚇 **Westminster/Waterloo**
Tel: 087-0990-8883

Get a bird's eye view of London on the 'Eye'! Located on the South Bank diagonally opposite the Houses of Parliament, the London Eye is Europe's largest Ferris wheel. It was only supposed to be a temporary attraction, but was so popular that it was made into a permanent one. Each 'flight' – i.e. one complete revolution of the wheel – takes about 30 minutes. The wheel moves slowly enough that passengers can get on and off without it ever having to stop. From the top, on a clear day, the view is amazing – and you can see Windsor Castle, about 40km (25 miles) away.

During holiday time, you might find long queues at both the ticket booth and to get on board. If possible, buy your tickets in advance at *www.londoneye.com* – it's quicker, and you can also get a discount by booking online. If you also want to skip the queue to get on, you may be interested in the fast track tickets. They aren't cheap, but you won't need to queue for more than 15 minutes before boarding. A word of warning – there are no toilets on the Eye, so make sure you go at the ticket office before your 'flight'!

MUST-DOS

COVENT GARDEN MARKET
Covent Garden, Westminster WC2
🚇 **Covent Garden**

Even if you hate shopping, chances are, you'll find something of interest in Covent Garden. Leave your big sister and your mother browsing through the fashion shops, and wander through the arts and craft stalls within the market – there's always a lot to look at. Once you've done that, check out the bookshop, the toyshops and gadget stores. **Pollock's** is a traditional toyshop which specializes in old-fashioned toys and puppet theatres, whereas the toys and gadgets in **Snook's** are decidedly more modern. There's even a **Disney** store and a **Games Workshop**, if that's what you're looking for. When you're done shopping, pop by the **Transport Museum** (pg 32) or watch the street entertainers. There are usually jugglers, acrobats and magicians around the square. Some are good, while others depend on comedy to make up for their lack of real skill, but they are always fun to watch!

After all that walking around, you'll probably be ready for a sugar hit. If you're not in the mood for the traditional sweet store or the cupcake shop in the market, take a seat at one of the many cafés and enjoy a scone and a cup of tea, or a milkshake and sticky cake, if that's more your scene. For an early lunch or dinner, we'd recommend **Wahaca** nearby – for yummy, tongue-tingling Mexican market food (pg 47).

THE SCIENCE MUSEUM
Exhibition Road, South Kensington SW7 🚇 **S. Kensington**
Tel: 087-0870-4868

There are so many fantastic museums, including the nearby **Natural History Museum** (pg 34) and the **V&A** (pg 33) right across the road, that it's hard to know which one to go to first!

The Science Museum is our favorite because there are so many fascinating things to look at, such as Stevenson's 'Rocket' – the first ever steam locomotive – as well as thousands of exhibits that show science in action.

The museum has been designed to appeal to all ages. The little kids in your family will love playing in The Garden gallery, while you'll find plenty of interesting interactive exhibits in the Launchpad gallery and the latest discoveries in the Antenna gallery. Once you've finished exploring all that, go to the Fly Zone to fly a fighter jet. Afterwards, visit the Force Field 4D Effects Theatre, where you will literally experience the smells, sights and sounds that the astronauts in the Apollo space mission endured! Challenge your parents to see if they can outwit the burglar alarm in the Secret Life of the Home exhibit, before going to watch a show on the huge IMAX 3D screen. There is plenty more to discover, but if you don't get to see it all, don't worry: you can come back another day – entry is free (there is a fee for the shows and the simulator).

ST PAUL'S CATHEDRAL
Ludgate Hill, City EC4M ⊖ St Paul's
Tel: 020-7236-4128

If you visit only one church in London, make it this one – it's spectacular! Located on the highest point in London, the cathedral, which is more than 300 years old, has the second-largest dome in the world. Go early, to beat the queues, and get the multimedia guide – it's full of such interesting facts that you'll be chasing your family around saying, "Hey, guess what?"

Once you've finished admiring the mosaics, statues and paintings, climb the dome – both inside and out. To reach the famous Whispering Gallery, you'll have to trek up 257 steps into the interior of the dome. It's well worth it though, as not only will you be able to see the magnificent painted frescos up close, you will also see how the gallery got its name. Ask your mother or father to stand opposite you on the other side of the dome. Follow the instructions posted in the gallery and

MUST-DOS

you should be able to hear them whisper from more than 40m (130 feet) away. This works best in the early morning before the cathedral becomes too noisy.

There are two galleries running around the outside of the dome too. The topmost one is called the Golden Gallery, and can be reached by a heart-pounding climb of 528 steps. You'll be rewarded with a fantastic view over London. The tourist opening hours are officially 8.30am–4pm, Mon–Sat, but as it's a working church it's worth phoning to check that the cathedral and the galleries are open on the day you want to visit.

THE MONUMENT

Monument Street, City EC3R ⊖ Monument
Tel: 020-7626-2717

If the climb up the dome in St Paul's Cathedral has left you feeling eager for more, go climb the 311 steps to the top of the Monument, which is located on the City side of London Bridge. The Monument was built to commemorate the destruction which occurred in the Great Fire of London. At 61m (202 feet) high, it is the tallest freestanding stone column in the world. If you make it to the top, you'll be rewarded with a certificate and fantastic views. Not recommended for toddlers. Open daily from 9.30am – 5.00pm.

Did you know?

The architect Sir Christopher Wren, who designed the Monument, also designed St Paul's Cathedral and 55 other churches too, after parts of London were destroyed by the Great Fire of London in 1666.

MUST-DOS

TOWER OF LONDON ✴
Tower Hill, Tower Hamlets EC3N ⊖ Tower Hill
Tel: 084-4482-7777

Step back in time at the Tower of London! The Tower has a long and blood-soaked history: it was a fortress and prison, a place of intrigue and murder, and the site of torture and executions. It was also once a royal palace, and as you wander through the splendid wood-paneled rooms, you'll be able to imagine what life was like in the royal court of King Henry VIII. Elsewhere, you'll see what it was like to work as a guard, or be locked up in the tiny dark prison cells, deep in the dungeons. If torture and weapons aren't your thing, visit the Crown Jewels – a glittering collection including a scepter (a large ceremonial rod-like item) that holds the largest cut diamond in the world.

Since 1485, the Tower and its prisoners have been guarded by retired soldiers called the Yeoman Warders (known more commonly as 'Beefeaters'). These days, they not only look after the Tower, its ravens, and the Crown Jewels, they also take tourists on short guided tours around the Tower. They're full of interesting stories, so it's worth joining one of their tours, if you have extra time.

London Duck Tours

Departs from Chicheley Street (near the London Eye), Waterloo SE1 ⊖ Waterloo
Tel: 020-7928-3132

Go for a ride in an amphibious vehicle (i.e. one that can drive down the street AND float on the water!). The Duck Tour, which takes about 75 minutes and includes a commentary, will take you around some of the major landmarks of Westminster before splashing into the Thames. The bright yellow 'tour bus/boat' is a converted military vehicle, of the type used in World War II. It's a little bit gimmicky, but fun – everyone always squeals with delight when the Duck drives down the ramp into the water!

London RIB Voyages (speedboat tour)

Departs from the London Eye Millennium Pier, Southbank SE1 ⊖ Westminster/Waterloo
Tel: 020-7928-8933

If you're a speed demon, you'll love the thrilling Ultimate Adventure Voyage. It will have you zooming by speedboat all the way from the **London Eye** to **Canary Wharf** (east London) and back again, in 50 minutes flat! There is also an 80-minute tour that takes you from the

London Eye through the Thames Barrier (flood barriers) all the way in **Greenwich** (pg 27), then back again. For a fast, but not-quite-as-fast alternative for families with tiny tots or grandparents, try the Captain Kidd's Canary Wharf Voyage. Wet weather gear is provided, and it's recommended you put it on, as you'll get wet from the spray, even on sunny days!

River Cruises

See the sights from the water on a leisurely river cruise. There are several companies that run river cruises along the Thames. One popular company is City Cruises. Tours depart from several piers along the Thames. If you want to get off along the way, you can get a River Rover card, which allows you to hop on and off at any pier, all day long. Check the website: *www.citycruises.com/riverred.htm* for more details, or call 020-7740-0400.

Tate to Tate

Tel: 020-7887-8888

Take a break from art, and whiz along the river! The Tate to Tate boat, which takes you from the **Tate Britain Museum** in Millbank SW1P (pg 37) to the **Tate Modern Museum** in Bankside SE1 (pg 36), or vice versa, is a bargain. The service, which is run by the Thames Clipper company, runs every 40 minutes throughout the day, during museum hours. You can buy tickets at the museum, or by calling the number above. Children under 5 ride free.

CROSSING THE RIVER THAMES

There are 33 bridges over the Thames in London! If you want to cross the river on foot, here are a few to choose from:

Tower Bridge

Tower Bridge is probably London's best-known bridge. It is the only bridge that can open up to let tall vessels sail underneath it! You can cross the bridge for free at street level, or for a fee via the top walkway. The view is great from the top, but it isn't cheap – included in the price is a short film and information about some of the sights you can see from on high. Cross this bridge if you want to go from the **Tower of London** (pg 11) to **HMS Belfast** (pg 32), or vice versa.

London Bridge

This bridge is dull to look at, but it's the best one if you want to cross from the **City** – which is London's financial district – to Bankside. On the City side, pay a visit to **Leadenhall Market** – a Victorian market featured in the *Harry Potter* films – then climb the **Monument** (pg 10), before crossing the Thames. On the other side, you'll find the full-size model of the Tudor warship – the **Golden Hinde** – as well as the **London Dungeons**, the **London Tombs** and the **London Bridge Experience** (pg 29/30).

ER

Millennium Bridge

This thin, pedestrian-only, steel suspension bridge was destroyed in the movie *Harry Potter and the Half-Blood Prince*. But luckily, in real life, it is still standing! During a charity walk, on the day after it was officially opened, the bridge started to sway from side to side, which earned it the nickname 'Wibbly Wobbly Bridge'. It was closed immediately afterwards for almost two years to fix the problem. These days, it is a safe and convenient way to cross the river if you've been to see **St Paul's Cathedral** (pg 8) and want to visit the **Tate Modern** contemporary art museum (pg 36/37) or to visit the reproduction of Shakespeare's Globe theatre on the south side of the river (recommended).

Westminster Bridge

You'll get a great view of the **Houses of Parliament** and **Big Ben** (London's famous clock tower), as you cross this bridge. Across the river is the impressive curved front of **County Hall**. It no longer holds offices, but instead contains a number of restaurants; two hotels; the **Movieum** (London Film Museum); and **Namco Station** – a video-game arcade, ten-pin bowling alley and a bumper car arena. However, we think the best attraction within County Hall is the **London Sea Life Aquarium** (pg 18). You can also buy tickets there for the **London Eye** (pg 6), which is located just outside, on the banks of the river.

ON THE WAT

Canal cruises:
London Waterbus Company

Departs from (1) Camden Lock NW1 (turn left where Camden High Street meets the canal) ⊖ **Camden Town; and (2) Brownings Pool (to the south, on Warwick Avenue side), Little Venice W9** ⊖ **Warwick Avenue/Paddington. Tel: 020-7482-2660**

A traditional canal boat, known in the UK as a 'narrowboat', is a lovely way to travel along Regent's Canal from Camden Lock (site of trendy **Camden Market** – pg 41) all the way to **Little Venice**, where you can visit the **Puppet Theatre Barge** (see below). You can do the journey in either direction, or buy a round-trip ticket. If you want, stop and visit **London Zoo** – you can enter the zoo by boat through a special gate so you can skip the queues at the main entrance!

Canal Museum
& Islington Tunnel boat trip

12-13 New Wharf Road N1 ⊖ **King's Cross St Pancras. Tel: 020-7713-0836**

When you visit this museum, you'll be glad you weren't a canal-boat worker! Learn about the history of the canals, and see how the canal-boat workers and their families lived. If you happen to be there on a Sunday during summer, book in advance to take the creepy, hour-long trip by narrowboat along the long, dark Islington Tunnel on Regent's Canal. The museum is closed on Mondays.

Puppet Theatre Barge

Oct to July: Moored at Little Venice, opposite 35 Blomfield Road, W9 ⊖ **Warwick Avenue**
Aug to Sept: Moored at Richmond, 83 Petersham Road TW10 ⊖ **Richmond. Tel: 020-7249-6876**
www.puppetbarge.com

Do something really different – watch a marionette show onboard a specially adapted barge! The Puppet Theatre Barge was started in 1982, and has entertained countless families and school groups since then.

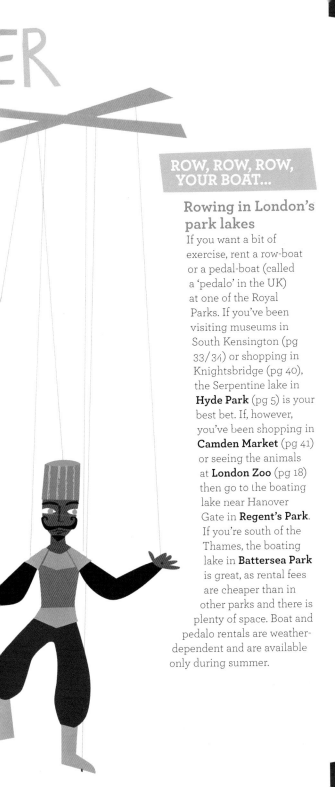

ROW, ROW, ROW, YOUR BOAT...

Rowing in London's park lakes

If you want a bit of exercise, rent a row-boat or a pedal-boat (called a 'pedalo' in the UK) at one of the Royal Parks. If you've been visiting museums in South Kensington (pg 33/34) or shopping in Knightsbridge (pg 40), the Serpentine lake in **Hyde Park** (pg 5) is your best bet. If, however, you've been shopping in **Camden Market** (pg 41) or seeing the animals at **London Zoo** (pg 18) then go to the boating lake near Hanover Gate in **Regent's Park**. If you're south of the Thames, the boating lake in **Battersea Park** is great, as rental fees are cheaper than in other parks and there is plenty of space. Boat and pedalo rentals are weather-dependent and are available only during summer.

TALK TO THE

London Sea Life Aquarium
G/F, County Hall, Westminster Bridge Road, Southbank SE1 ⊖ Westminster / Waterloo
Tel: 087-1663-1678

Leave London behind as you enter darkened corridors lit with the eerie green glow of the tanks. Wander around the fourteen different 'zones' and see all the fascinating creatures that live in the oceans, rivers and streams around the world. You can also get a close-up look at a shark's belly or its fearsome teeth, as you travel in the glass tunnel along the bottom of the shark tank!

ZSL London Zoo⚔
Regent's Park, NW1 ⊖ Camden Town
Tel: 020-7722-3333

Did you know that London Zoo is one of the world's oldest zoos? Although the elephants and rhinos that lived there in the past have been moved to a more roomy sister zoo (Whipsnade Zoo in Bedfordshire), there are still tons of creatures to see. Some live in enclosures which have been carefully built to look like their natural habitat, such as the Rainforest Life attraction. The zoo website recommends buying the entry ticket online on its website (*www.zsl.org*) to avoid queues, but another way to get in is to go by waterbus – with a zoo/canal trip combined ticket (pg 16). You get a nice lazy ride down the canal and you don't have to brave the crowds at the gate – it's a win-win situation!

ANIMALS

Hyde Park Stables
63 Bathurst Mews, Bayswater W2
⊖ Lancaster Gate. Tel: 020-7723-2813
Go horse riding in the center of London! Book in
advance to ride a pony or horse (with an instructor)
around Hyde Park. Suitable for both experienced
riders as well as those with no riding experience.
The weight limit for adults is 79kg/ 175lbs, and
children must be aged 5 or more. Riding hats and
boots are supplied free of charge.

Stag Lodge Stables
Kingston Vale, Richmond SW15 ⊖ Putney Bridge
(then take bus 85 towards Kingston)
Tel: 020-8974-6066
One of several stables operating at Richmond Park
(which is also a deer park – pg 24/25), Stag Lodge
Stables is a well-established family-run business, with
horses suitable for experienced young riders, as well
as Shetland Ponies for children over 3 years old. Call to
book in advance. Hats and boots can be borrowed.

DOMESTICATED CREATURES

Horse Guards
Horse Guard Parade
⊖ Westminster/Charing Cross
Watch the horse guards ride their beautifully trained
and groomed horses in this very traditional ceremony.

Like the Foot Guards at Buckingham Palace, the Horse Guards have a daily changeover ceremony. They ride from **Hyde Park Barracks**, down the Mall, to Horse Guard Parade in Whitehall. The ceremony takes place at 11am every day (but at 10am on Sundays) by the arch of the Horse Guard Building.

Vauxhall City Farm
**165 Tyers Street, Vauxhall SE11 ⊖ Vauxhall
Tel: 020-7582-4204**
If you're visiting the **Imperial War Museum** (pg 32) and need a break from the horrors of war, pop over to this small farm for some furry and fluffy therapy. From 10.30am–4pm every Wednesday through to Sunday, you can see about 80 animals – from the usual farmyard animals (sheep, pigs, cows, ducks and horses), to the small and fluffy (rabbits and guinea pigs) to the more unusual (alpacas and ferrets). Call for more details. Entry is free, but donations are welcomed and encouraged. Closed Monday and Tuesday.

Mudchute Farm & Park
**Pier Street, Isle of Dogs, Tower Hamlets E14
⊖ Canary Wharf, then take the DLR to
Crossharbour Station, followed by a 10-minute walk.
Tel: 020-7515-5901.**
This is the biggest urban farm in Europe. The huge green space is home to hundreds of farm animals (from fat pigs to llamas with movie-star eyelashes!). You can also get a nice breakfast, lunch or afternoon tea at the Mudchute Kitchen, which sells homemade food. Mudchute hosts a number of indoor and outdoor activities for families throughout the year. Call or check the website (*www.mudchute.org*) for details. Visitors are welcome from Tue–Sun, 9am–5pm.

URBAN WILDLIFE

Richmond Park
Details on pg 24/25
Apart from the hundreds of deer that roam this park,

ANIMALS

you may spot rabbits, foxes, shrews, mice, voles, and many different birds, as well as nine species of bat. There are over 500 different types of butterfly and over 1300 different types of beetle living there too.

Hyde Park & Kensington Gardens
Details on pg 5/26

Hyde Park, and Kensington Gardens next door, is not only home to tons of squirrels, but also to a large number of waterfowl – some of which nest on an island in the middle of the lake. You'll see sleek ducks, snooty swans, comical moorhens, and fierce Canadian geese. The geese and swans have a reputation for being bad tempered, so don't get too close to them!

Did you know that all unmarked mute swans (a native species) in England are considered to be the Queen's property?

Take a walking tour of Westminster & Southbank
See map on pag 62/63

If you're feeling fit, see the sights on a walking tour! Start your journey at **Buckingham Palace** (pg 4) and walk down **The Mall**, making a small detour down Marlborough Road to take a peek at **St James's Palace** (see below), before returning to The Mall. If you want a break, pop into St James's Park for lunch, snack or afternoon tea in the excellent **Inn on the Park** restaurant (pg 43). Continue down The Mall to **Trafalgar Square** to see Nelson's column, then turn down Whitehall past the end of **Downing Street** – the house at number 10 is the home of the British Prime Minister! Carry on until you reach the **Houses of Parliament** where you'll see the famous **Big Ben** clock tower. You can then either take a detour and visit **Westminster Abbey**, or head straight over Westminster Bridge to the **Southbank**. Once there, you can visit the **London Aquarium** (pg 18) and the **London Eye** (pg 6), or continue on to see other attractions on the south side of the river!

Changing of the Guard ceremony
Takes place at Buckingham Palace, St James's Palace (Marlborough Road), and Wellington Barracks (Birdcage Walk), Westminster SW1

The Royal Palaces are guarded by five different regiments of guards. Each regiment takes 24-hour shifts to guard Buckingham Palace and St James's Palace. Every day during the summer, at around 11am, the regiment on duty hands over to the next regiment, in a ceremony called the Changing of the Guard.

During the ceremony, the guards on active duty march in formation in the forecourt of Buckingham Palace, and in Friary Court on Marlborough Road – just off Pall Mall – in nearby St James's Palace. The new regiments form ranks in the forecourt of Wellington Barracks, on Birdcage Walk, before marching to both palaces to take over. Although the ceremony is longer (and often includes a marching band!) at Buckingham Palace, the crowds are usually heavy and it is difficult to see anything, so unless you are there early to get a good spot, we recommend you go to Friary Court to watch the ceremony at St James's Palace instead. The schedule of the ceremony can be found on *www.royal.gov.uk* (under 'Royal Events and Ceremonies'/'Changing the Guard') or call 020-7766-7300.

Somerset House
& Edmond J. Safra Fountain Court
Strand, Westminster WC2R  **Temple or Covent Garden. Tel: 020-7845-4600**

Somerset House may be famous for the performances, exhibitions and shows that are held there all year round, but our favorite part of it is outside – in the Fountain Court. In the summer, you might get a refreshing surprise as you walk across the courtyard, in the form of a sudden spray of water squirting out of the ground! During the winter, the fountains are off, but the courtyard is transformed into a magical outdoor ice skating rink. Call the number above to find out when the fountains are on, or, if you're there in the winter, to book a time for the ice skating rink.

Kew Gardens
Richmond, Surrey TW9 ⊖ Kew Gardens
Tel: 020-8332-5655

If you'd like to see some exotic plants (you'll find both the smelliest and the largest plant in the world, as well as a tree which is about 250 years old!), giant stag beetles, or the view from a treetop walkway, then Kew Gardens is a good place to go. In addition to acres of beautiful gardens, there are several huge glasshouses – such as the Palm House and the Temperate House – where you can climb up to the elevated galleries and look down on the plants; the peaceful Waterlily House; and the ultra-modern Alpine House which uses environmentally friendly technology to keep it cool. If you get tired, hitch a ride on the Kew Explorer – a hop on/hop off land-train. You can actually stay on it all the way round, for a 40-minute guided tour! If you're interested in learning more, ask about other guided tours which are suitable for older kids and adults, or get the guidebook for kids aged 7–11. Younger kids, aged 3–9, will like the indoor playzone called Climbers and Creepers. Kew Gardens is open every day (apart from Christmas Eve and Christmas Day) from 9.30 am.

Richmond Park
Richmond TW10 ⊖ Richmond

Richmond Park is a National Nature Reserve and is home to over 600 Red and Fallow Deer, which graze freely around the ancient oak trees. If you're lucky you'll also be able to spot rabbits, foxes, shrews, mice, voles, and many different birds, as well as several species of bat. There are over 500 different types of butterfly and more than 1,300 different types of beetle living there. But it's not all about the wildlife, there's lots here for humans too: two playgrounds – at the Kingston and Petersham gates (to the top left and bottom left of the park) – two cafés and several refreshment points. You can go horse riding (see **Stag Lodge Stables**, pg 19), or cycling: rent a bike at the car park near Roehampton Gate (call **Park Cycle** at 070-5020-9249 for details of what you need, prices and opening times). If you are over 10 years old, you can try your hand at Power Kiting! Call **Kitevibe** at 020-7870-7700 if you want to learn how to operate a 2-line kite; or, if you know how to operate a 4-line kite, ask about their kite-buggy riding or land-boarding lessons!

Kensington Gardens 🚫
& Princess Diana Memorial Playground
**Top left corner of Kensington Gardens between
Orme Square Gate / Black Lion Gate W2**
⊖ Queensway

Kensington Gardens, which is nestled tight against
the western edge of **Hyde Park**, was the private garden
of **Kensington Palace**, which is within it. Although
it's possible to go on a tour of Kensington Palace,
the younger members of your family would probably
be more interested in the Princess Diana Memorial
Playground which is open to kids aged 12 or below.
The playground has a Peter Pan theme. It features a
pirate ship on a 'beach', as well as teepees, and all sorts
of other things to explore. There are also toilets, plenty
of seats and a café nearby for when you need a break.
The playground opens at 10am and closes when it
starts to get dark – 3.45pm during winter months, and
7.45pm May–August. It is closed on Christmas Day.

Fat Tire Tours 🚴
Tel: 0788-233-8779

Take a tour on two wheels! This company takes small
groups of tourists around London on two different
cycling tours. The first takes you through the royal
parks to **Westminster**, while the other takes
you over the **Thames**, via Tower Bridge.
The Royal London tour is suitable
for all ages (all sizes of bikes are
available including adult bikes
with child seats attached for
tots), but the Thames Bike
Tour is a little more
challenging and

the participants have to be over 5 feet (152cm) tall. The tours are between four and five hours long and involve lots of stops (including one for lunch) so are not as tiring as the long timescale would suggest. Call for more details or to book.

Greenwich

Trains to Greenwich SE10 (in SE London) leave from London Bridge, Charing Cross and Waterloo East. If you're interested in space or naval history, there's a lot to see and learn in Greenwich (pronounced *gren-itch*), which is home to the **Maritime Museum**, the **Royal Observatory** and the **Peter Harrison Planetarium**. Discover why it was so important that accurate time-keeping instruments be invented, and how explorers managed to draw precise maps. Get a photo of yourself with one foot in the western hemisphere and one foot in the eastern, by standing with a foot on either side of the Prime Meridian – a metal line in the ground of the Royal Observatory. You can also watch one of the spectacular shows at the planetarium, before strolling (or rolling, if you're not worried about grass stains) down the hill and through the park into town.

There's an **open-air market** in the centre of town which sells food on Wednesdays, antiques on Thursdays and Fridays, and all sorts of things at the weekend – but even if you're not interested in the stalls, there are two shops (open daily) around the outside which you'll find worth the visit: **Compedia** at 10 Greenwich Market is a toyshop that specializes in games and puzzles, and right next door is **Mr Humbug** – a sweetshop filled with all sorts of old-fashioned sweet favorites.

IT'S RAINING,

CINEMAS

There are a lot of cinemas all over London, but your best bet is probably to head down to Leicester Square – not only are there four cinemas actually inside the square, there are another six nearby. You can find out what's showing by reading the cinema listings in a newspaper or a copy of *Time Out* magazine.

Science Museum IMAX 3D Theatre
Take a break from exploring the Science Museum, and be transported to exotic places around the world in 3D! See pg 7/8 for more details on the museum.

BFI London IMAX 3D Theatre
1 Charlie Chaplin Walk, South Bank, WaterlooSE1
⊖ **Waterloo**
Tel: 020-7199-6000
See the latest 3D releases plus 3D movies that take you into the depths of the ocean or far out into space on the largest screen in England! Call for details on show times.

THEATRES

Theatres in London are fantastic and feature everything from musicals to comedy to drama. For a listing of shows suitable for the younger members of the family, go to this website and click 'family', 'children', or 'general' for all shows: *www.officiallondontheatre.co.uk/london_shows/age*. If you haven't already booked the tickets, get half-price tickets (for West End shows being performed that day or the next) at the **TKTS** booth in the middle of Leicester Square (it's the one with a little clock tower). Beware of buying them from other discount booths or from touts (scalpers); they often charge a booking fee, and the tickets may not be valid.

IT'S POURING

CHILDREN'S THEATRES

Polka Theatre
240 The Broadway, Wimbledon, London SW19
⊖ South Wimbledon. Tel: 020-8543-4888
Polka has been putting on shows and workshops for kids for thirty years! Call to find out what's playing. You can get to the Polka Theatre by taking the Northern Line Underground train to South Wimbledon. From there, it's just a five-minute walk.

Puppet Theatre Barge
See a marionette show on a specially converted barge on Regent's Canal. See pg 16/17.

THEMED ATTRACTIONS

The London Dungeons
28-34 Tooley Street, London Bridge SE1
⊖ London Bridge. Tel: 020-7403-7221
Actors dressed in period clothes will make you shiver, with gory tales about Jack the Ripper, Sweeney Todd (both murderers!), and the Great Fire of London. The London Dungeons and its competitor (London Bridge Experience / London Tombs) across the street, are both quite expensive and you will probably have to stand in line to get in. The Dungeons are dark and atmospheric, and some parts might make you jump, but if you're hoping for a fright, you may find it a bit tame. Not recommended for very young children and anyone who dislikes long lines, or has a fear of enclosed spaces. You can get a discount by booking online at *www.the-dungeons.co.uk*.

IT'S RAINING,

The London Bridge Experience & London Tombs

2-4 Tooley Street, London Bridge SE1

🚇 **London Bridge. Tel: 0800-043-4666**

This attraction is split into two parts: the London Bridge experience takes you on a 20-minute historical 'tour' led by costumed actors, where you will learn about London Bridge's history, as well as the Great Fire of London. The first part is more educational than frightening, but the London Tomb part which follows is more scary – as you shuffle through the dark, hanging onto the shoulders of the person in front, the actors dressed as zombies leap out at you unexpectedly. If you like Halloween horror houses, then you may enjoy this, but it isn't recommended for young children, for those who hate queuing or who have a fear of enclosed spaces. Book online for big discounts: *www.thelondonbridgeexperience.com*.

Madame Tussaud's

Marylebone Road, Marylebone NW1

🚇 **Baker Street. Tel: 0871-894-3000**

If you like seeing waxwork figures of pop stars, actors, athletes and historic figures, then you'll enjoy Madame Tussaud's. But be warned, the attraction is quite expensive, generally very crowded (which makes the figures hard to see, and involves a lot of queuing) and you may not recognize the older 'stars' featured. However, if you don't mind going around 5–5.30pm you might be able to get some 'Late Saver' tickets online. Only a limited number of these tickets are available each day, so book in advance at the website: *www.madametussauds.com/London*. As well as the tickets being half price, it is generally less crowded late in the day. Warning: There are a couple of parts which may not be suitable for younger children or sensitive souls!

IT'S POURING

INDOOR FUN

Queens Ice and Bowl
17 Queensway, Bayswater W2 ⊖ Queensway
Tel: 020-7229-0172
Whirl on the ice, or send the bowling pins flying at this center, which is a few minutes from Hyde Park. You can rent all the equipment (including ball ramps and lightweight balls for younger bowlers) but don't forget to bring a pair of socks. The bowling alley only has 12 lanes so if you're determined to bowl, call in advance to make sure there isn't a tournament on. There's also an ice-cream parlour with homemade gelati, Belgian waffles, pizzas and other snacks.

Gambado
7 Station Court, Townmead Road, Chelsea SW6
⊖ Imperial Wharf. Tel: 020-7384-1635
If it's raining and your mother is desperate for somewhere she can take your younger brother or sister to let off steam, this huge indoor adventure play center – for kids up to age 10 – is a good place to head. It has a giant play frame, climbing walls, dodgem (bumper) cars, a carousel, organized activities, plus a deli with healthy food and coffee for your parents. Be warned though, you will have to pay a one-off registration fee the first time you go, as well as the normal entry price. Call for opening times and prices.

London Transport Museum
Covent Garden Piazza, Westminster WC2E
⊖ Covent Garden. Tel: 020-7565-7299
This little museum is fun to visit – especially if you
like buses, trains and trams! There are lots of things to
examine, from the horse-drawn cart of 200 years ago, to
the amazing models showing how they built the world's
first underground rail network (known as the 'Tube') and
how the Tube tunnels were used in the war. There are
lots of interactive displays – and you can board many of
the vehicles on display. There is a modest entry fee for
adults but children under 16 (accompanied by an adult)
go free.

Imperial War Museum ✏
Lambeth Road, Lambeth SE1 ⊖ Lambeth North
Tel: 020-7416-5000
Even if you are not a war buff, there will be probably be
something of interest for you here. There is a life-sized
replica of a World War II era house with bomb shelters,
a walk-through section about the trenches (with all the
noises, and smells you would have encountered), and a
section about the children (called evacuees) who were
sent away to the country for months, away from the cities
that were likely to be bombed. For those who like tanks
and planes, there are plenty of those on display too.
Entrance is free, with a charge for special exhibitions.

HMS Belfast
Morgan's Lane, Tooley Street, Bankside SE1
⊖ London Bridge. Tel: 020-7940-6300
This museum ship, which is permanently
moored on the southern bank of the
Thames opposite the **Tower of London**,
saw active service in WWII and in the
Korean War. Visitors get a fascinating
glimpse of what it was like to be on it
during times of war – a section of the
ship has been restored so you can see
not only the living quarters, but the sick
bays, the chapel, the kitchens, and even
the laundry area. Descend into the bowels

of the ship to see the engine room and the boiler –
before going to visit the command areas and the guns.
There is a modest entrance charge for adults, but there
is no charge for children under 16 with an adult.

Victoria and Albert Museum (V&A)
Cromwell Road, South Kensington SW7
🚇 South Kensington. Tel: 020-7942-2000

The V&A is one of the three grand old museums in
South Kensington. Unlike the non-arty Natural History
and Science Museums, the V&A is a museum of design
and decorative arts. It has a collection spanning
5,000 years – which includes prehistoric art, as well as
paintings, photographs and sculptures. You can also
see all sorts of weird and wonderful styles of furniture,
toys and fashions! You'll wonder how ladies managed
to move around in such elaborate and uncomfortable-
looking dresses, marvel at the way-out costumes worn
by modern-day rock-and-roll superstars, and giggle at
the clothes that were popular when your parents or your
grandparents were teenagers! Entrance is free.

British Museum ✩
Great Russell Street WC1B 🚇 Tottenham Court Road/Holborn. Tel: 020-7323-8299

If you are a history freak, you'll be in heaven in the
British Museum, which has a collection ranging
from Ice Age art (a beautiful carving of reindeer on a
mammoth tusk), to Egyptian mummies (it has one of

the largest Ancient Egyptian collections in the world), to treasures from Ancient Greece, the Middle East and the Far East. There are some terrific multimedia guides available – which will tell you interesting snippets about select objects in various galleries, and will bring history to life. There is one multimedia guide for kids aged 5–10, as well as a longer one for teens and adults. Entrance is free.

Natural History Museum
Cromwell Road, South Kensington SW7
🚇 **South Kensington. Tel: 020-7942-5011**
Remember to say "hello" to 'Dippy' the enormous replica of a Diplodocus skeleton which is located within the main hall, before going to see the rest of the museum. There's a lot to explore – from the Mammal Halls (which contain almost every mammal you can think of, including a life-size model of a blue whale); to the futuristic Climate Change Wall; or the Cocoon in the Darwin Centre, where, among other things, you can watch real scientists at work. In other parts of the museum, you can find out about the Earth – from the fiery hot core to the crust on which we live – or study the human body in depth. You can even listen to the kinds of noises a baby hears from within its mother's womb! There are a lot of interactive activities to keep you busy too. Entrance is free, although there is a charge to get into some of the special exhibitions.

Science Museum
See pg 7/8.

VIA

Museum of London
150 London Wall, City EC2Y ● Barbican
Tel: 020-7001-9844
If you're curious to discover what London is about, this is the place for you! The museum has galleries with information about the the original Roman settlement, the Great Fire of London, and even the present-day city. Not only are archaeological items displayed, there are also galleries that trace fashion trends – see what your grandparents might have worn in the Swinging Sixties, and compare that to what the Punks wore! The museum is open daily from 10am–6pm. Admission is free.

Pollock's Toy Museum
1 Scala Street, Fitzrovia W1T ● Goodge Street
Tel: 020-7636-3452
Ever wondered what an old-fashioned toy shop might have looked like? Well, wonder no more! Make your way around the small, somewhat dusty rooms and the twisty staircases to look at all the old toys they have on display here. There's something interesting crammed in every corner. There are some boys' toys but because there are a lot of dolls, this museum may appeal more to girls. Open 10am–5pm Monday to Saturday, except on Bank Holidays.

Ragged School Museum
46-50 Copperfield Road, Bow, Tower Hamlets E3
● Mile End. Tel: 020-8980-6405
Think your school is tough? Wait till you see what life was like for pupils in 1870s England!

Named after a charity school (The Ragged School), this museum is in one of the original school buildings. Inside, you'll find a Victorian classroom, with slate boards to write on, and dunce hats for those who get their answers wrong. The museum is only open to the public on Wednesday, Thursday (both 10am–5pm) and on the first Sunday of each month between 2pm–5pm. If possible, visit on a Sunday, as you will have the chance to experience a lesson with a strict teacher! There are two sessions starting at 2.15 and 3.30. Each lasts for 45 minutes. Everyone – even your parents – is welcome, but there's only room for 34 people so make sure you put your name down for it as soon as you get to the museum! Afterwards you can have a drink at the café, and examine the Victorian kitchen on site.

National Gallery
Trafalgar Square, Westminster WC2N
Charing Cross. Tel: 020-7747-2885
Where can you go on a detective hunt, search for royalty or act like a know-it-all? At the National Gallery, of course! We'd highly recommend the family audio tours – in particular *Teach Your Grown-Up About Art*. Once you've done the tour (which lasts about an hour), you can try the worksheets which are full of quizzes and jokes. For those who want serious in-depth info about the art, there are free 10-minute talks, as well as one-hour guided tours. On Sundays, there are free workshops for kids aged 5–11, as well as free morning 'magic carpet' storytelling sessions for the under 5s. During holiday times there are also free workshops for those aged 12–17. Space is limited so make sure you check the schedule in advance via their website (*www. nationalgallery.org.uk*) or by phone, and get to the Education Centre Foyer earlier than the stated start times! Museum entrance is free.

Tate Modern
Bankside SE1 Southwark or London Bridge
Tel: 020-7887-8888
Some people love and 'get' modern art. Others consider it a load of nonsense! Whatever your opinion, you'll

agree that the building (an old power plant) housing this museum is grand, and there are a lot of intriguing things to see! There are family trails and children's multimedia guides, which are recommended as they are fun to follow as well as informative. Entrance is free but a small donation is requested.

Tate Britain
Millbank SW1P ⊖ Pimlico
Tel: 020-7887-8888

The Tate Britain is packed full of British art – from the old masters to modern-day artists. If you're there between October and January, you might catch the Turner Prize exhibition. The Turner Prize is awarded to the best of modern British art – so you will see some interesting (and odd) things in that show! At the weekend (11am–5pm), there are free Art Trolley sessions at which you can create a piece of art, and also some family trails for the under-5s to follow. If you feel like going to both the **Tate Modern** and the Tate Britain in one day, take the **Tate to Tate boat ride** on the Thames (pg 13). Entrance is free.

LONDON DAY

Hampton Court Palace
**Hampton Court, East Molesey,
Surrey KT8
Tel: 0844-482-7777**

This palace is a bit out of the way – but
it's fairly easy to get to (take a train
from Waterloo Station) – and it's worth
the journey. You'll feel like you've taken
a trip back in time – to Henry VIII's
court. You can follow the family trail,
or better still, join one of the regularly
scheduled tours led by costumed
guides. Explore the great banqueting
hall, as well as the enormous kitchens
which were used to prepare meals for
hundreds of people, twice a day. (If
you're lucky, you might even see some
Tudor food being cooked.)

Hampton Court is said to be haunted
by King Henry's six wives. We've
never seen any ghosts, but depending
on when you are there, you may see
a jousting or falconry show, or even a
recreation of Henry's marriage to his
sixth wife. There's a lot to see indoors
– but make sure you leave enough time
to go in the huge maze in the garden.
It's more tricky than it seems, so
prepare to get lost! If you'd like to see
some videos about life in Tudor times,
or to book tickets online (it's slightly
cheaper that way), go to *www.hrp.org.uk/
HamptonCourtPalace*.

Chessington World of Adventure
**Leatherhead Road, Chessington,
Surrey KT9
Tel: 087-0444-7777**

We think there's tons of exciting stuff to
do in Central London, but if you're the

TRIPS

type who can't stand a vacation without thrill rides, then you should visit Chessington. Travel by train from Waterloo Station to Chessington South, and you're a 10-minute walk away. Within the park are different themed 'lands' – with rides and animal attractions designed to appeal to different ages from tots to adults. Chessington is popular so go early and expect long lines. You can book tickets online for a discount (*www.chessington.com*) and there is an express pass, if you hate standing in line.

Legoland ⚔
Winkfield Road, Windsor SL4
Tel: 0871-2222-001

If you're not so keen on scream-inducing rides or you have younger brothers and sisters, you might want to try Legoland rather than Chessington – there's a rollercoaster and some thrill rides, but in general, the attractions are more about fun than fear. If it's warm, pack a swimsuit and towel and get soaked in the Waterworks. Remember to stop by Miniland – where nearly 40 million LEGO bricks have been used to recreate scenes from around the world – and watch a 4D movie. Book your tickets online (*www.legoland. co.uk*) to get a discount, or buy a ticket that includes rail travel and a shuttle bus from the station. You can get more details at London Waterloo or Paddington Stations.

Harrods 🛍

**87-135 Brompton Road, Knightsbridge SW1X
🚇 Knightsbridge. Tel: 020-7730-1234**

If you're looking for bargains, you won't find many in Harrods – but even if you aren't a millionaire, it's worth spending time in this famous (and HUGE) department store. Visit the food halls, then head straight upstairs to the toy and games rooms, where even the adults and older teens will find something new and exciting! There's a bookshop, designer clothing, and departments selling everything else. Freshen up in the 'luxury toilets', before going to one of the many cafés. Open Mon–Sat 10am–8pm and on Sunday from 11.30am–6pm.

Hamleys ✓ 🛍 🛍

188-198 Regent Street W1B 🚇 Oxford Circus or Piccadilly Circus. Tel: 0871-704-1977

Hamleys, which was established in 1760, is one of the largest toyshops in the world! There are seven floors to explore, packed with everything from traditional toys and games to the modern and electronic. The magic displays and the toy demos will keep your parents interested while you browse. Open Mon–Fri 10am–8pm, Sat 9am–8pm, and Sun 12pm–6pm.

Bookshops ✗

There are many branches of **Waterstones** and **WH Smiths** bookshops, but our favorite is **Foyles**. The main store is at 113–119 Charing Cross Road, Westminster, WC2H. Tel: 020-7437-5660. Comics and manga fans may like **Gosh! Comics Bookshop** (39 Great

u DROP

Russell Street, Bloomsbury WC1B. Tel: 020-7636-1011) but many of its books are for adults.

GOOD SHOPPING AREAS

Oxford Street (West End)
A very long street! Visit **Topshop** and **H&M** for cool fashions, and explore bookshops, places selling games and music, plus several department stores like the famous **Selfridges**. Plan your shopping expedition before you go at: *www.oxfordstreet.co.uk*

Regent Street (West End)
Mostly designer clothes shops here. Visit **Paul Smith** and use the elevator – it's fun! **Hamleys** is also on this street ... don't miss it, whatever you do.

King's Road (Chelsea)
Lots of trendy fashion shops, bookshops, record shops, and quirky shops selling novelties.

Brompton Road (Knightsbridge)
Mostly expensive designer gear – but you might want to stop by and have a look at **Harrods** (see opposite).

Covent Garden
See pg 7.

Camden Lock Market
Trendy but grungy! Full of cutting-edge fashions and quirky little shops. Stick together; it's easy to get lost!

Westfield Shopping Mall
If you all like different shops, then **Westfield Shopping Mall** might be a good choice. With over 260 shops, plenty of restaurants, and kids' activities on the weekend (such as storytelling at **Foyles** bookshop, discounted morning cinema tickets, and face-painting), every member of your family should be able to enjoy themselves for a few hours! Take the Underground to Shepherd's Bush – it is a short walk from the station.

FOOD, GLORI

There are tons of decent restaurants in London. We can't list them all, so we've recommended a few good chains with dependable grub (that's slang for 'food'!), places that serve traditional British food such as fish and chips, pie and mash (mashed potatoes), high tea, as well as a few interesting restaurants with unusual food.

Patisserie Valerie

Several locations: Kensington Church Street; Duke of York Square near Sloane Square; Motcomb Street, Belgravia (a few roads behind Harrods); Great Cumberland Place near Marble Arch; Bedford Street, Covent Garden (check www.patisserie-valerie.co.uk)

Looking for a good place to stop for breakfast, lunch or a snack? Try a branch of Patisserie Valerie, or Paul Patisserie (see opposite page). Here you can have a sinfully delicious cake, a scrumptious pastry or a yummy sandwich. Or, if you're not that hungry, a cup of soup and a delicious salad. These cafés are popular, so expect to line up if you go at peak times!

OUS FOOD

Paul Bakery and Patisserie

Several locations including: Brompton Road; Covent Garden; Fulham Road; Gloucester Road; King's Road; Marylebone High Street; Regent Street; Thurloe Street, South Kensington; Paternoster Square, St Paul's (check www.paul-uk.com)

One look at the cakes and tarts in the window, and you'll be tempted! Most Paul bakeries have a nice seating area, in which you can enjoy their delicious sandwiches, quiches, pizzas, salads and wonderful desserts. Perfect for breakfast, lunch or a snack.

Busaba Eathai – Thai restaurant

Various locations including: Panton Street, next to Leicester Square; Bird Street, near Selfridges on Oxford Street; and Wardour Road in Soho, close to Oxford Street (check http://busaba.com)

The Busaba Thai restaurants have long shared tables and simple bench seats, but that's the only similarity to a school cafeteria. The food is yummy – there are spicy items for chilli fans, as well as mild dishes. The service is fast, and best of all it's really good value so your parents will be pleased too! Pop by for lunch or an early dinner – if you go late you might have to queue. Open 12pm–late.

Inn the Park Restaurant Café

West of Horse Guards Parade, St James's Park, Westminster 🚇 St James's Park
Tel: 020-7451-9999

This restaurant-café, which overlooks the lake, is well disguised and hard to see from some angles, as it is partly buried in a grassy hillock! Once you've found it though, you'll enjoy the food and the peaceful setting. If you want to sit in the sun to enjoy your sandwich, a slice of cake or tea, take your tray to the terrace or the roof. You can also choose to eat something a bit more filling from the breakfast, lunch/dinner or afternoon tea menu – the gourmet selections are sure to make your mouth water. Open 9am–8pm in the summer, 10am–4pm in winter.

Roast

The Floral Hall, Borough Market, Stoney Street, Southwark SE1 ◉ **London Bridge / Borough**
Tel: 084-5034-7300

The restaurant, which is in the historic Borough Market, specializes in traditional British food – from a 'Full English' breakfast, to Scotch egg (a yummy snack or starter featuring a boiled egg coated in sausage meat and breadcrumbs, then fried), to meltingly tender roast beef with Yorkshire pudding (popovers) and all kinds of other tempting choices. The restaurant isn't cheap but the food is of a high standard, as is the atmosphere – and the views! It's also family friendly, with kids' menus and even stuff to draw with if you get bored. Call for opening times, and to book a table.

The Golden Hind

73 Marylebone Lane, Marylebone, Westminster W1U ◉ **Bond Street**
Tel: 020-7486-3644

There are a lot of restaurants that boast that they are the best 'chippy' (fish and chip shop) in London, but this one always makes it into top-ten lists, due to the good food! The fish (delivered fresh every day) is fried in a lovely crispy batter and the chips are crispy on the outside and meltingly soft on the inside, just the way they are supposed to be. Eat it the English way, with lashings of malt vinegar, salt, and a side order of mushy peas! Open Mon–Fri 12pm–3pm, then again 6pm–10pm. On Saturday it is open 6pm–10pm. Closed on Sundays.

Rock & Sole Plaice ✷

47 Endell Street, Covent Garden WC2H ◉ **Covent Garden. Tel: 020-7836-3785**

This traditional fish and chip shop has been around for about a hundred years. The nice thing about this place, is that when it's sunny you can sit outside to enjoy your food. Warning – the large portion of the fish is very large! They do have children's portions too, if you're not very hungry. Open until 11pm.

OUS FOOD

The Cadogan Arms
298 King's Road, Chelsea SW3 🚇 **Sloane Square/
South Kensington. Tel: 020-7352-6500**
This modern-looking pub calls itself a 'gastropub',
which means 'a pub that serves great food'... and that's
exactly what it is. In addition to the adventurous
choices which will make the parents happy, they have
nice simple food like pasta, burgers or sausages and
mash, cooked well and with good ingredients. Its
location on hip and trendy King's Road will make the
shoppers in your family happy too!

The Friend at Hand Pub
4 Herbrand Street, Bloomsbury WC1N
🚇 **Russell Square. Tel: 020-7837-5524**
Tucked around the corner from Russell Square station,
and minutes away from the British Museum (pg 33/34),
it's one of the few traditional pubs that welcomes
families. It's not award-winning or anything, but you'll
be able to get some decent 'pub grub' – think sausage
and mash, pie and mash, fish and chips – while Dad
tries some 'real ale', the traditional English beer!

The Wolseley
160 Piccadilly, Mayfair W1J 🚇 Green Park/ Piccadilly Circus. Tel: 020-7499-6996
OK the bad news first: it's expensive and you have to book in advance. But if breakfast is your favorite meal, it might be worth splashing out for one at the Wolseley, which has been voted one of the best places for breakfast (and high tea) in London. Despite the grand atmosphere, they welcome families, and they'll treat you like royalty!

St James's Tearoom at Fortnum & Mason
181 Piccadilly, Westmister W1A
🚇 Green Park/Piccadilly Circus
Tel: 020-7734-8040
There are a lot of lovely hotels in Mayfair – such as the **Dorchester**, **Ritz**, **Claridge's**, and the **Connaught** – which are famous for their traditional and formal high teas. But if you want something a little more casual, try the St James's Tearoom or the Fountain Tea Room in the famous Fortnum & Mason food shop. They have been long known for the lovely tea and edible treats they sell – try a cuppa with a scone, or indulge in the high tea menu.

Cockney Pie & Mash Shop
314 Portobello Road, Notting Hill W10 🚇 Ladbroke Grove
Tel: 020-8960-9409
Pie and mash shops are not meant to be posh – and this one certainly isn't – but it's authentic down to the name, as pie and mash was very popular with the Cockneys in the East End of London! As well as various types of pie and mashed potatoes (served with a thick green parsley sauce called 'liquor'), you can also get sausages and mash and stewed eel – which is an acquired taste! Filling food, at a good price. Open daily, 10am–6.30pm.

OUS FOOD

M Manze Pie & Mash ✗
87 Tower Bridge Road, Bermondsey, Southwark SE1
🚇 **Borough. Tel: 020-7407-2985**

This place is the oldest pie and mash shop in London – it's over 120 years old! It only sells jellied eels (a vinegary boiled eel dish) and freshly baked minced beef pie or the vegetarian equivalent which uses soy 'mince'. Both pies are served with mashed potatoes and a choice of gravy or liquor. We'd recommend the gravy, unless you particularly like parsley. It's said that many famous people drop by – so keep your eyes peeled for the likes of footballer David Beckham! The opening times vary, but you'll be safe if you aim to be there between 11am–2pm. Closed on Sundays.

Wahaca
66 Chandos Place, Covent Garden WC2N
🚇 **Covent Garden**
Tel: 020-7240-1883

Are you ready to tickle your tastebuds? Mexican food in England has a reputation for being greasy and blah but you won't find that in Wahaca! The Mexican market food they serve is not all spicy, but it's really delicious – share a selection of tacos, tostadas, and crispy taquitos, or, if you're starving, have a burrito. But don't forget to leave room for a crispy hot churro (similar to a donut) dipped in yummy chocolate sauce. You can't book, so we recommend you arrive early, as the cheap and delicious food attracts large crowds and long queues!

FOOD, GLORI

Food for Thought
31 Neal Street, Covent Garden WC2H
🚇 **Covent Garden**
Tel: 020-7836-0239

Vegetarian food has a bad reputation for being tasteless and way too ... um, 'vegetably', but that won't be a problem here. This is the type of vegetarian restaurant that even meat-eaters will agree to come back to! Get there early though, as it is tiny – and don't forget to save some room for the oh-so-delicious desserts – such as banoffee pie (a divine banana, toffee and cream pie), Missisippi mud pie or some traditional apple crumble.

Nice Green Café
Cecil Sharp House, 2 Regent's Park Road, Camden Town NW1 🚇 **Camden Town**
Tel: 020-7485-2206

If you've been visiting Camden Lock Market or Regent's Park, and you're looking for a place with yummy homecooked food, why not consider the Nice Green Café? You might have to search a little to find this café, which is tucked away in a large hall (the headquarters of the English Folk Dance and Song Society) near the northeastern corner of Regent's Park, but if you've worked up an appetite looking for it, you won't be disappointed! The café serves mouthwatering dishes, such as chunky homemade soups, savory pies and yummy sandwiches, along with delicious breads and cakes that are baked there, every day. Open Mon–Sat, 10am–4pm.

Benihana Chelsea/

Piccadilly

77 King's Road, Chelsea SW3 🚇 **Sloane Square**
Tel: 020-7376-7799
37 Sackville Street, Piccadilly W1S 🚇 **Piccadilly**
Circus. Tel: 020-7494-2525

We'd be the first to admit that this is not a gourmet Japanese restaurant. It's not cheap either, but for a tasty (and very large) lunch or dinner set with a 'show', this is a fun place to go! You'll be seated around a large Teppan – steel grill – on which your personal chef will cook you dinner. Knives, pepper shakers and bits of food go whirling through the air, expertly juggled by your chef, who may also challenge you to catch bits of steak that he flicks at you, with your mouth! The food will sizzle, and the onion-ring mini-volcano will belch flames as you laugh and eat. A fun meal!

FAST FACTS

- London is the capital city of the United Kingdom (which includes England, Scotland, Wales and Northern Ireland).

- The city was established about 2000 years ago, in 47AD by the Romans, who named it Londinium. Within fifty years, despite a war and several fires, it was the biggest city in Roman Britain.

- There are many Roman remains in London – one of the best known is London Wall, a defensive wall that the Romans built around Londinium. You can still see part of it in what's now the financial district. The road that runs along its remains is also known as London Wall (see Museum of London, pg 35).

- Around 7.5 million people live in Greater London, and almost 15 million people from other countries visit it each year. That's twice as many visitors as there are inhabitants!

- The currency of the UK is the pound sterling, which most people just call 'the pound'. It is divided into a hundred pence – often pronounced 'pee' – so £2.10 is 'two pound ten pee'.

- London weather is very changeable, and the only guarantee is that it'll be cold between November and February! Temperatures in summer can soar to over 30°C (85°F) but then the next day, it might rain and plunge down to 10°C (50°F). So take lots of layers that you can pile on or peel off, as needed. This is even a good idea in winter, as stores, trains and hotels tend to be (over) heated, even if it's cold out.

- On average, it rains most between September and February, but a fold-up umbrella in your luggage is a good idea, whenever you go!

SPEAK THE LINGO

Wait a minute, don't they speak English in London? Yes they do, but if you're not from here, you may not know all the terms used. See how many you recognize!

Talking food ...

Bangers and mash : fried sausages (usually pork) and mashed potatoes.

Biscuit : baked treat, small, sweet and often crunchy. Similar to a cookie, but not as roughly shaped. Sometimes called a 'biccy'.

Brekkie : slang for 'breakfast'.

Candyfloss : cotton candy.

Fancy a cuppa? : Would you like a cup of tea?

Chips : french fries – often cut into wide strips, and served with malt vinegar and salt.

Crisps : potato chips.

99 Flake : soft-serve ice-cream served in a cone, with a small flaky chocolate bar stuck into the ice-cream.

High tea : meal served mid-afternoon, often featuring crustless sandwiches, cakes and scones (see pg 52).

Jacket potato : baked potato.

Jelly : gelatin dessert, known in the USA as 'Jello'.

Lolly/ice-lolly : candy lollipop/ice popsicle.

Mincemeat : sweet mixture of dried fruits such as raisins, currants and mixed peel. Hamburger meat, however, is called 'mince' or 'minced meat'.

Pasty : a small pie-like object, covered in pastry.

Pudding : usually a steamed dish – can be savory or sweet. Occasionally used to mean 'dessert'.

Rock (food) : candy shaped like a rod.

Scone : round, soft and halfway between cake and bread. Often eaten with jam and cream for high tea. Similar to what Americans call a 'biscuit'.

Spud : slang for 'potato'.

Sweet : candy, sometimes used to mean 'dessert'.

Toad in the hole : a savory dish of sausages baked in a Yorkshire pudding.

Yorkshire pudding : baked savory batter – similar to 'popovers' in the USA.

In other words ...

Bloke : slang for man – "that bloke just trod on my toe".

Bobby : affectionate nickname for policeman. 'Copper' is the slang term.

Brolly : short for 'umbrella'.

Boxing Day : the day after Christmas Day.

Bum : slang for 'bottom'!

Cab : taxi.

Cheerio : another way to say 'goodbye'.

Chemists : a drug store.

Dressing gown : bathrobe.

Dodgems : bumper cars (a fairground ride).

Fiver (money) : five pounds.

Fortnight : two weeks.

Footie : soccer – also called football in the UK.

Guard (on a train) : the conductor.

Jumper : sweater (a warm, often woollen top).

Knickers : girls' underpants.

Loo : slang for toilet – also called the 'lav', 'WC' or 'the bog'.

Mobile : short for mobile-phone or cell-phone.

Nappy : diapers.

Pants : in the UK this ALWAYS means underpants – outerwear is called 'trousers'.

Pavement : sidewalk (pedestrian area at side of road).

Quid : slang for sterling pound (money).

Rubbish : an expression of disgust. Also means garbage.

Ta : short for 'thanks awfully'!

Telly : short for television.

Tenner (money) : slang for ten pounds.

Tube : slang for the London Underground rail system.

Zebra crossing : a crosswalk (pedestrian crossing).

LONDON KNO

HOW TO TRAVEL AROUND LONDON

- London has a good public transportation system. The three main systems are: (1) the London Underground or 'the Tube', which has trains that run mainly underground (surprise!); (2) the National Rail system, which connects London to the suburbs and beyond; and (3) the London bus service. If you're in the mood for door to door transport, you can always catch a taxi (which are generally black in color), but be warned, they're not cheap!

- If you are visiting London for an extended time (or if you go often), and plan to use public transport a lot – your parents might want to get an Oyster Card. This is a pay-as-you-go stored-value card that allows you to travel on any Underground, rail, or bus within London, without the hassle of having to take coins, queuing and buying a ticket. Each journey ends up being a lot cheaper, too, if you pay by Oyster. There is also a maximum amount you can spend per day – after you reach that limit, you can ride for free for the rest of the day. At the end of your trip, you can get a refund on any credit (money) left on your Oyster card, or you can simply put it away for the next trip! Ask at any Underground or train station about them.

- If your parents don't want an Oyster, they can get a one-day travelcard. It gives you unlimited trips on the Tube, bus and trains within London, for that day. Hint: if you're planning to get a one-day travelcard on a weekday, buy it after 9.30 am, to get a discount. You can get travelcards for longer periods than one day, but if you think you might buy one every day for a week or more, it might be better to get an Oyster card instead. Ask at any Underground or train station about travelcards.

- Kids aged 10 and under, traveling with an adult, can ride on many Tube and bus routes for free – ask the guard standing near the ticket gates to let you through.

- For kids of 11+ the cheapest way to travel is by buying a travelcard. Kids travelcards are cheaper than adult cards. Ask at any Underground or train station for details.

- It's hard to figure out how to pronounce some London destinations. Here is a rough guide: Euston: *You-stun*, Fulham: *Ful-lam*, Gloucester: *Gloss-ter*, Leicester: *Less-ter*, Marylebone: *Marly-bone*, Southwark: *Suth-thuck*, Tottenham: *Tot-nam*.

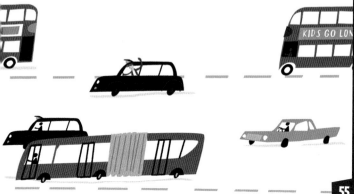

There has been a bridge across the Thames – near the site of the present-day London Bridge – since Roman times. The bridge you see nowadays was built in 1973. The bridge that stood there before the present one was about 140 years old when it was sold to an American collector. He took it apart, labeled all the stones then shipped the pieces back home, where it was rebuilt in Lake Havasu City, Arizona, USA.

◀ Write an interesting fact you find in here

Because of a superstitious belief that 'the kingdom will fall' if all the ravens (big black birds, related to the crow) leave the Tower of London, the resident ravens have the feathers of one wing clipped to stop them from flying far. This doesn't harm the birds but keeps them unbalanced during flight.

Trafalgar Square used to be full of pigeons. In the past, over 30,000 lived in and around the square. Worried about damage caused by pigeon droppings to the buildings nearby, the government made it illegal to feed the birds in 2007, and now you'll see very few pigeons there!

London has the largest populaiton in Eurpue it also has one of the worlds largest toy stores hamleys and the worlds largest Ferris wheel London eye

Write an interesting fact you find in here

When people talk about Big Ben, they normally mean the clock tower of the Houses of Parliament. But actually, the name belongs to the largest bell within the clock tower, which has the official name of 'Great Bell of Westminster'!

MAKE A NOTE

Make a note of your best London memories and experiences here!

yum!

COOL

Hamley has 7 levels full of toys, inside they have a yogourt shop and build-A-Bear workshop. On the Lower ground levle they have outdoor items and customer services, on the ground levle cuddly toys Puppets (there is more then that), the first floor has thing for babeys, the second floor has every kind of doll imaganble, the floor caled the third floor has Arts, craftes, board games, card games and the Loveable huggable build-A-bear, the fourth floor buzz with remote control toys, the fifth and final floor has the washrooms (very important facilty) and LOL (Lots of Lego. and that's hamley's for you packed with fun, cheerfulness and Love

KEEPSAKES

Stick pictures and tickets, or draw here!

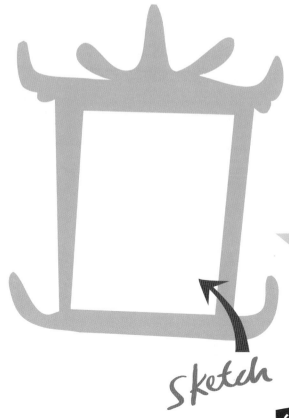

Sketch

GO WALK ABC

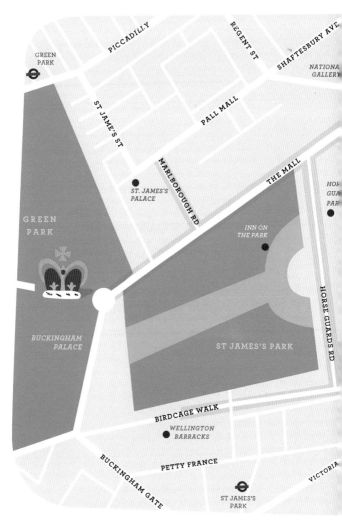

LONDON is great fun to walk around. There are a lot of lovely green areas, beautiful buildings, and interesting sights to see. Our **suggested walking tour** (pg 22) takes in many well-known sights of London. The walk will take about an hour, including sightseeing stops. When you are done, you have the option of visiting the **London Eye** (pg 6). But if you're still